THE HAMPTONS
The Delaplaine 2020 Long Weekend Guide

Andrew Delaplaine

NO BUSINESS HAS PAID A SINGLE PENNY OR GIVEN *ANYTHING* TO BE INCLUDED IN THIS BOOK.

GET 3 **FREE** NOVELS
Like political thrillers?
See next page to download for 3 FREE page-turning novels—no strings attached.

Senior Editors
Renee & Sophie Delaplaine
Senior Writer
James Cubby

Gramercy Park Press
New York London Paris

WANT 3 **FREE** NOVELS?

If you like these writers--
Vince Flynn, Brad Thor, Tom Clancy, James Patterson, David Baldacci, John Grisham, Brad Meltzer, Daniel Silva, Don DeLillo

If you like these TV series –
House of Cards, Scandal, West Wing, The Good Wife, Madam Secretary, Designated Survivor

You'll love the **unputdownable** series about Jack Houston St. Clair, with political intrigue, romance, suspense.

Besides writing travel books, I've written political thrillers for many years. I want you to read my work! Send me an email and I'll send you a link where you can download the 3 books, **absolutely FREE.**

andrewdelaplaine@mac.com

Copyright © by Gramercy Park Press - All rights reserved.

THE HAMPTONS
The Delaplaine Long Weekend Guide

TABLE OF CONTENTS

Chapter 1
WHY THE HAMPTONS? – 5

Chapter 2 – WHERE TO STAY – 17
High on the Hog – Sensible Alternatives – Budget

Chapter 3 – WHERE TO EAT – 34
Extravagant – Middle Ground – Budget

Chapter 4 – NIGHTLIFE – 65

Chapter 5 – WHAT TO SEE & DO – 70

Chapter 6 – BEACHES – 75

Chapter 7 – SHOPPING & SERVICES – 81

INDEX – 89

OTHER BOOKS BY THE SAME AUTHOR – 92

Chapter 1
WHY THE HAMPTONS?

Only because there's nothing quite like the Hamptons. Visiting Long Island in the summer is just one of those things everybody ought to do once.

It gets a little crazy (OK, it gets a *lot* crazy) in the height of the hectic summer season, with bumper-to-bumper traffic in East Hampton and elsewhere, but

it's still something you ought to experience. I always prefer to go a couple of weeks before it gets too nuts, or the week right after Labor Day, when everybody skedaddles back to New York or wherever they came from. And believe me, it does clear out with the snap of a finger right after Labor Day.

A couple of years ago, I spent two weeks in a beach house a couple of miles east of Westhampton.

The first week was before Labor Day and the second week was after Labor Day, and unless you've experienced that particular part of the summer up here, you can't appreciate how drastically (and quickly) the area changes.

When I was in my 20s, broke and eking out a subsistence living working in retail at Saks Fifth Avenue in Manhattan, I spent all the long dreary winter months doing my damnedest to make friends with people who had places out in the Hamptons, working every angle I could, whether involving business or pleasure—to wrangle as many invitations as I could squeeze out of my friends.

Then, of course, those long hot Fridays would roll around and you'd have to make your way out to the island to take up your friends on those invitations.

It was often a nightmare getting out to the Hamptons because every way to get there was a tedious chore, endlessly exasperating. Sometimes I'd take the train, the **Long Island Railroad**.

Other times I'd hop a ride with friends doing the same thing I was—mooching off pals with pads out on the island. We'd split the cost of the gas and endure the backed up traffic on the Long Island Expressway (LIE). Every Friday you wonder why they call it an "expressway," because it's everything but "express." You only want to take a car if you need it to get from town to town. Otherwise, try to avoid having a car in season.

Overhead you'd occasionally see helicopters ferrying the rich and famous to their summer estates. (Those choppers are still flying.) If you have the money, you can fly out in one of them.

You don't have to be one of the rich folks who own the big mansions—filmmakers like Spielberg, hedge fund managers, etc.—to enjoy the Hamptons, but it's always nice to know a few of them.

If you've ever visited Newport, you've seen how the mega-rich robber barons lived in the Gilded Age at the end of the 19th Century. Well, the robber barons alive today don't go anywhere near Newport. The Hamptons constitute the Newport of today. In the height of the summer season, they're all here. They are the ones who are getting into the restaurants and nightlife hot spots you can't.

And I'd like for you to think about including the Hamptons when you think about off-season traveling. I'd been going there for 20 years before I made my first trip out there in the winter. A destitute writer friend had a housesitting gig out in East Hampton and over a three-month period from March to May I had to go out to meet him twice a week to work on a screenplay we were putting together. I can't tell you how wonderful the towns are off-season. The resident populations are very small. Everybody knows everybody else. It's a very small-town vibe that is very welcoming.

When I first began my travel writing career decades ago, I was told by an old pro that one of the best trips to make in the U.S. was a drive with a lover up the Maine coastline, with little stopovers here and there, wherever chance took you.

He was right.

But the same thing can be said of the Hamptons.

However you get there, or whenever you go, prepare for a unique experience that can't be duplicated anywhere.

LONG ISLAND RAILROAD
www.mta.info/lirr

HAMPTON JITNEY
www.hamptonjitney.com

HELICOPTER SERVICE
www.zipaviation.com

HAMPTON HOPPER
www.hamptonhopper.com
PRICE: varies
    A new app-based transportation service that offers a convenient and affordable way to get round the Hamptons, with stops from Sag Harbor to Montauk on a Thursday through Sunday schedule. Their signature green buses travel between the villages of the Hamptons so you can hop on and off. Daily unlimited-ride passes available.

Traditionally, there are really two towns that make up what the world calls "The Hamptons," and they would be Southampton and East Hampton. But I would enlarge the definition to include (moving from west to east):

WESTHAMPTON. Like a lot of little villages out here, this one has the quaint and charming town center that the minute you see it makes you want to move here. But the real attraction is the endless miles of pristine beaches.

QUOGUE. One of my absolute favorite towns in the Hamptons. It's ever-so-small, but wander along the tree-lined streets and admire the old houses. Maybe you'll want to move here, too.

HAMPTON BAYS. A great place to stop to look at all the boating traffic.

SOUTHAMPTON. The Old Lady of the Hamptons. This is where a lot of the Old Money lives. You'll know who they are by the high hedges lining the streets. They don't want their pictures taken. The *Nouveau Riche* might be able to buy big houses here, but they can't get into the exclusive clubs. Excellent shopping. Hell, excellent everything.

WATER MILL. Has some of the best restaurants in the area. See the pumpkins in the picture above?

BRIDGEHAMPTON. More excellent shopping, with an emphasis on antiques. The prices are outrageous as a rule, so this makes a great place to browse without buying. (Or, if you're visiting during the end of the season, you can pick up bargains they don't want to hold till next summer.)

SAGAPONACK. More excellent beaches. Farm stands make buying produce fun again.

WAINSCOTT. Home to a lot of very wealthy people. Some of the most expensive real estate in the country, but that can be said of all the Hamptons.

EAST HAMPTON. The crown jewel of the Hamptons. This is where it's hardest to get a table, where the traffic is the worst, where you can't even squeeze into a nightspot, but where you'll want to try. Shopping, famous people on every corner, excellent restaurants and shops.

AMAGANSETT. Further on is one of my favorite places. When I was young, I visited a famous film director's house right here on the beach. It was a big spread and there were lots of fabulous beautiful people. They were snorting cocaine in large salad bowls. I tried it. It was good.

"What is this?" I asked.

"You're from Miami and you've never had coke before?"

Well, I hadn't. What did I know?

The parties still rock n roll, however, though the director is dead.

I went to my first real clam bake on the beach here.

MONTAUK. My Aunt Sallye Delaplaine lives out here in the summer. I don't venture out this far as a rule. In the winter it's one of those austere places that give new meaning to the word "windswept."

SAG HARBOR. On the North Fork is my second-to-favorite town, Sag Harbor, home to the

American Hotel and one of the best bars in all the Hamptons. Lots of writers live out here in the summer, hob-nodding with each other and comparing their publishing advances and literary awards. It's hard to imagine now, but Sag Harbor used to be an important whaling center.

SHELTER ISLAND. Take a ferry or hire a boat to get out here. It's worth the trip. Better yet, stay out here. Everything's much cheaper than on the mainland.

Chapter 2
WHERE TO STAY

1770 HOUSE RESTAURANT & INN
143 Main St, East Hampton, 631-324-1770
www.1770house.com
Located in a three-story house built in the mid-1600s. The house features 7 guest rooms each with a sitting room. There are two in-house restaurants: The Tavern and The Inn. Amenities include: free breakfast, free Wi-Fi, and free parking. Note: No elevator so suitcases should be lightweight.

THE AMERICAN HOTEL
49 Main St, Sag Harbor, 631-725-3535
www.theamericanhotel.com
Built in 1846, this is one of Sag Harbor's landmark buildings. This elegant boutique hotel offers eight beautifully appointed guest rooms. The restaurant here consistently wins awards for its 3,000 or so labels. The food is French, but with an American twist. The bar is packed with a Who's Who in the busy summer season. Amenities include: Free breakfast and free Wi-Fi. On-site restaurant, spa, and public rooms with large screen TVs.

THE ATLANTIC HOTEL
1655 County Road 39, Southampton, 631-283-6100
www.atlantichotelsouthampton.com
This hotel offers 68 oversized rooms, different sizes according to your needs. Amenities include: Free breakfast, free Wi-Fi, and free parking. Facilities

include swimming pool and wheelchair access.

THE BAKER HOUSE 1650
181 Main St, East Hampton, 631-324-4081
www.bakerhouse1650.com

As the most exclusive Bed & Breakfast in the Hamptons, the luxurious Baker House offers beautifully decorated rooms, each with a lavish private bath. Amenities include: minibar, flat screen TV, iPod dock, full cable services & DVD, and free Wi-Fi. Most rooms have wood-burning fireplaces and whirlpools. Breakfast is served daily in the breakfast room or in the beautiful garden. Facilities include English gardens, outdoor infinity-edge pool, and The Baker Spa (complimentary for all guests).

BARON'S COVE
31 W Water St, Sag Harbor, 844-227-6672
www.baronscove.com
NEIGHOBORHOOD: Sag Harbor
What once was a beat up motel has been upgraded into a fine family-friendly hotel offering 67 village and harbor facing rooms and suites. John Steinbeck used to live not far down the road and often frequented the bar here. The porch of the restaurant overlooks the marina. Amenities include: Complimentary Wi-Fi, flat-screen TVs, and minifridges. Some have decks and/or gardens. Complimentary breakfast, bikes, parking, and beach shuttle. On-site American restaurant. Features include: outdoor saltwater pool, tennis courts, gym and yoga classes. Dog-friendly rooms available.

BEACHCOMBER RESORT AT MONTAUK
727 Old Montauk Hwy, Montauk, 631-668-2894
Dune Resorts Management Group
www.beachcomber-montauk.com
This resort offers beautiful accommodations with most rooms featuring gorgeous views of the ocean. Amenities include: Free Wi-Fi, tennis court, heated swimming pool, sauna, and private desks.

BEACH PLUM RESORT
779 Old Montauk Highway, Montauk, 631-668-4100
www.beachplumresort.com
This resort is a boutique co-op rental community that offers studios one and two bedroom units and cottages. Every unit is individually decorated and equipped by the owners containing basics like cooking utensils. Amenities include: Direct beach access, free Wi-Fi, in-ground heated pool, and private decks. Conveniently located across from the ocean, and walking distance from the Village of Montauk.

BOWEN'S BY THE BAYS
177 West Montauk Highway, Hampton Bays, , 631-728-1158
www.gobowens.com
This resort offers a variety of accommodations: elegant guest rooms and private cottages (one, two, or three bedrooms). Facilities include: swimming pool, playground, shuffleboard court, putting green, and lighted tennis court. Conveniently located in the heart of the Hamptons, near the ocean and bay with activities like fishing, golf, mini-golf, petting zoo, aquarium, water park and outlet shopping. Free parking. Pet-friendly resort.

A BUTLER'S MANOR
244 N Main St, Southampton, 631-283-8550
abutlersmanor.com
NEIGHOBORHOOD: Southampton

Elegant, 1860 colonial-style guesthouse offers five individually-designed guestrooms each with private bathrooms. Amenities include: Flat screen TVs, CD and MP3 players, and complimentary Wi-Fi. Complimentary breakfast served in the garden. Beautiful property set on lush landscaped gardens surrounding a full-sized salt-water swimming pool. Conveniently located near local dining, shopping, and beach opportunities.

THE CROW'S NEST INN
4 Old West Lake Dr, Montauk, 631-668-2077
www.crowsnestmtk.com
Located about a mile and a half east of Montauk, this inn offers 14 renovated king rooms, each with a private deck over-looking Lake Montauk. Amenities include: Free parking, Wi-Fi, and "New York Times" delivery. Excellent restaurant on-site (chicken skewers with harissa comes with delicious yogurt). Have a cocktail by the fire pit and enjoy the water view. Within walking distance of Ditch Plains beach. Recently added lake front cottages now available.

HAMPTON MAID INN
259 E Montauk Hwy, Hampton Bays, 631-728-4166
https://hamptonmaid.com
NEIGHBORHOOD: Hampton Bays
Quaint inn set on 5 acres overlooking the Shinnecock Bay features 29 guest rooms. Amenities include: Complimentary Wi-Fi and flat-screen TVs. Facility features include: outdoor pool, sundeck, wood gazebo overlooking the pool, and country-style breakfast restaurant on-site.

DRIFTWOOD ON THE OCEAN
2178 Montauk Highway, Montauk, 631-668-5744
www.driftwoodmontauk.com
This family-friendly resort offers 52 studios and one-bedroom guest rooms. Amenities include: picturesque grounds, free Wi-Fi access, swimming pool, fitness center with gym, and free parking.

HARBORSIDE MOTEL
371 West Lake Dr., Montauk, 631-668-2511
http://www.montaukharborside.com/
This motel offers clean and tasteful guest rooms, studios, and suites. Amenities include: cable TV, free Wi-Fi, and continental breakfast served on weekends during summer season. Facilities include: swimming pool two professional all-weather tennis courts, bar/lounge, and free parking.

HEDGES INN
74 James Lane, East Hampton, 631-324-7101
www.thehedgesinn.com
This 12-room inn overlooks the beautiful village pond. The inn is a landmark and home to the famous swans that return year after year. Amenities include: free breakfast, free Wi-Fi, and free parking. On-site bar/lounge. Conveniently located near Main Beach.

THE INN AT WINDMILL LANE
23 Windmill Lane, Amagansett, 631-267-8500
www.innatwindmilllane.com
This Inn offers a complex that features three privately-gated cottages set in a beautiful landscaped garden. Amenities include: Free gourmet continental breakfast, daily New York Times, Beach parking passes, Beach cruisers, chairs, coolers, umbrellas and towels, free Wi-Fi, flat screen HDTV, iPod docking station, and private steam room with shower. Facilities include a common room with gourmet kitchen. Shuttle service to local attractions.

C/O THE MAIDSTONE
207 Main St, East Hampton 631-324-5006
www.themaidstone.com
The Maidstone offers 19 individually designed rooms and cottages with a giant living area. Amenities include: organic coffee, stocked minibar, Continental Scandinavian breakfast buffet (in keeping with the bright and cheerful Nordic design applied to this 18th century Hamptons icon), free yoga in the Buddha Garden (summer only), and beach parking permit. Other perks include bikes (Kronan bikes, adapted from bikes used by the Swedish Army), DVD library, concierge service, spa services available, and on-site gift shop.

THE MONTAUK BEACH HOUSE
55 S. Elmwood Ave, Montauk, 631-668-2112
www.thembh.com
Located in the heart of downtown Montauk, this 32-room boutique hotel offers a friendly social atmosphere with two pools (where people hang out late into the night), and two bars always open. Onsite restaurant/bar by the pool. Free Wi-Fi and breakfast. Cast iron beds & claw foot tubs. Free parking. Non-smoking rooms available.

MONTAUK YACHT CLUB
32 Star Island Rd, Montauk, 631-668-3100
montaukyachtclub.com
NEIGHBORHOOD: Montauk
Resort overlooking Lake Montauk offering 106 nautical designed guest rooms, villas and suites. Amenities include: Complimentary Wi-Fi, flat-screen TVs, coffeemakers, minifridges, private balconies or patios. Facilities include: fitness center, sauna, indoor and outdoor pools, tennis courts, spa, two restaurants, a bar and lounge. Access to sailing courses, boat excursions and menu of family activities. Gift shop. Complimentary shuttle service.

RUSCHMEYER'S
161 Second House Rd, Montauk, 631-668-2877
www.ruschmeyers.com
Popular spot featuring 19 luxury, cabin-inspired rooms that may remind you of summer camp. Located on 3 acres of lush, lakeside woodland. Free Wi-Fi and parking. Pet friendly. Non-smoking hotel. On-site restaurant (Tuesday is burger nght), lounge

and nightclub. Activities available from yoga to ping pong.

SOLE EAST RESORT
90 2nd House Rd, Montauk, 631-668-2105
www.soleeast.com
This hip little resort features 67 comfortably appointed rooms that feature flat screen TVs and iPod docks. Climate controlled rooms, Aveda bath products, and free Wi-Fi. Poolside & garden-side cabana suites available. Weekend pool parties with guest DJ, BBQ and cocktails. Pet friendly.

SOUTHAMPTON INN
91 Hill St, Southampton, 631-283-6500
www.southamptoninn.com
NEIGHBORHOOD: Southampton
Tudor-style hotel offering 90 guest rooms. The restaurant here, **Claude's**, will set up a clambake for you if you ask them. Amenities include:
Complimentary Wi-Fi, flat-screen TVs with cable, minifridges and work stations. Facilities include: on-site restaurant, meeting space, library with Steinway piano, heated outdoor pool, lawn games, tennis court, and private gardens. Complimentary shuttle to Cooper's Beach. Wheelchair accessibility.
Conveniently to nearby golf, boating, fishing, surfing, kayaking, biking, shopping, restaurants, galleries, parks, and museums. Pet-friendly rooms available.

SUNSET BEACH
35 Shore Road, Shelter Island, 631-749-2001
www.sunsetbeachli.com

NEIGHBORHOOD: Shelter Island
A favorite of the young elite crowd, this beachfront hotel offers 20 guest rooms with private decks. Amenities include: Complimentary Wi-Fi, HDTV, DVD players, stereos with CD player, iPod docks, Kol Design bath products, and complimentary bikes. Facilities include: outdoor showers, beach boutique, spa, French bistro, bar, game room and library. No pool.

THE SURF LODGE
183 S Edgemere St, Montauk, 631-483-5041
www.thesurflodge.com
Built in 1967, this popular lodge offers a comfortable destination for travelers. The lodge offers 19 airy rooms with ocean views. This is one of Montauk's hotspots so be prepared for a party atmosphere. On-site restaurant. Free parking. Set on Fort Pond, this boutique hotel offers beach-chic rooms and suites.

Amenities include: free Wi-Fi, TVs, iPod docks, and private decks. Guests mingle on the waterfront deck that features a bar with live music. Popular among families and international travelers. Willie Nelson and Courtney Love have performed on the deck.

TOPPING ROSE HOUSE
One Bridgehampton-Sag Harbor Turnpike, Bridgehampton, 631-537-0870
www.toppingrosehouse.com
This is a very charming 22-room inn situated in an 1842 Greek Revival mansion catering to the wealthy. The historic house is flanked by a modern addition with sleek interiors and exteriors. There's the awful nuisance of the backed up traffic on the Montauk Highway, but they have solved the problem with blackout curtains and soundproof windows. You can look at the traffic, but you won't hear it from your room. Full breakfast included, as well as many other amenities. Perfectly located—just a short walk from the Hampton Jitney and a bike ride to the beaches. One of the best restaurants in the area is here.

Chapter 3
WHERE TO EAT

75 MAIN
75 Main St, Southampton, 631-283-7575
www.75main.com
CUISINE: American/Italian
DRINKS: Full Bar
SERVING: Breakfast, Lunch, Dinner, Open daily
PRICE RANGE: $$$
A popular spot that offers great food and features a nightclub vibe at night where you'll find music and dancing. The lounge is a popular hangout and the food is incredible. Here you'll dine on great pastas or excellent dishes like Blue Crab Crusted Halibut and

Crispy Red Snapper. Popular with A-listers and celebrities.

ALMOND
1 Ocean Rd, Bridgehampton, 631-537-5665
www.almondrestaurant.com
CUISINE: French
DRINKS: Full Bar
SERVING: Dinner
PRICE RANGE: $$$
NEIGHBORHOOD: Bridgehampton
Comfortable bistro offering traditional French fare. Menu favorites: Steamed black mussels with shallots and Roasted Chicken. Raw bar.

AMAGANSETT SEAFOOD STORE
517 Montauk Hwy, Amagansett, 631-267-6015
www.amagansettseafoodstore.net
CUISINE: Seafood Market
DRINKS: Beer & Wine
SERVING: Open daily
PRICE RANGE: $$$
Known for selling the freshest fish in the area. Shop for items to take home or snack here. Great selection of seafood like lobster rolls, fish tacos, seaweed salad and even lobster mac and cheese. A locals' hangout on Saturdays.

THE AMERICAN HOTEL
49 Main St, Sag Harbor, 631-725-3535
www.theamericanhotel.com
Built in 1846, this is one of Sag Harbor's landmark buildings. This elegant boutique hotel offers eight

beautifully appointed guest rooms. The restaurant here consistently wins awards for its 3,000 or so labels. The food is French, but with an American twist. The bar is packed with a Who's Who in the busy summer season. Amenities include: Free breakfast and free Wi-Fi. On-site restaurant, spa, and public rooms with large screen TVs.

ARBOR
240 Fort Pond Road, Montauk, 631-238-5430
www.arbormontauk.com
CUISINE: Mediterranean
DRINKS: Full Bar
SERVING: Dinner Wed – Thurs; Lunch & Dinner Sat & Sun; closed Mon & Tues
PRICE RANGE: $$
NEIGHBORHOOD: Montauk
Casual chic eatery with a beautiful exterior and surrounded by lush gardens. Interior features a sunken dining room, a 30-foot bar, and a private room with a wine cellar. Menu features farm-to-table selections. Menu picks: Cucumber and Crab and Octopus Risotto. Nice wine selection.

BABETTE'S
66 Newtown Ln, East Hampton, 631-329-5377
www.babettesrestaurant.com
CUISINE: Seafood/Vegan
DRINKS: Full Bar
SERVING: Breakfast & Lunch – Mon, Thurs - Sun, Dinner Fri & Sat
PRICE RANGE: $$$
NEIGHBORHOOD: East Hampton

Billed as "an eclectic cutting edge restaurant," this eatery focuses on local, seasonal organic products. Large menu with creative vegetarian fare (no 'real' meat served here) and seafood. Outdoor patio, juice bar, and creative cocktails. Pet-friendly. No reservations for breakfast or lunch.

BEACH BAKERY CAFÉ
112 Main St, Westhampton Beach, 631-288-6552
www.beachbakerycafe.com
CUISINE: Bakery
DRINKS: No Booze
SERVING: Open daily from 6 a.m.
PRICE RANGE: $$$
Located in the center of the village of Westhampton Beach, this bakery sells it all, including croissants, donuts, muffins, cookies, and bagels. Their café menu includes items like lasagna, pizza, soups, cakes, pies, tarts and pastries. Try their specialty Three King Pie (a combination of apple, peach raspberry and blueberry).

THE BELL & ANCHOR
3253 Noyac Rd, Sag Harbor, 631-725-3400
www.bellandanchor.com
CUISINE: Seafood/American (New)
DRINKS: Full bar
SERVING: Dinner; closed Tues
PRICE RANGE: $$$
NEIGHBORHOOD: Sag Harbor
Upscale, seafood-centric eatery offering lovely bay views. Favorites: Pan Seared Scottish Salmon and

Pan Roasted Dorade. Very popular. Reservations recommended.

BISTRO ÉTÉ
The Mill Center
760 Montauk Hwy, Water Mill, 631-500-9085
https://www.bistroete.com/
CUISINE: French
DRINKS: Full Bar
SERVING: Dinner; closed Mon & Tues.
PRICE RANGE: $$$
NEIGHBORHOOD: Water Mill
Casual eatery in a cute little cottage offering French classics in an elegant if somewhat Spartan interior. Feels very much like you're in the Hamptons off season when locals are the only customers. (I could eat here every night because the food, while simple, is so painstakingly prepared from the best ingredients.) I like the shiny little light fixtures and almost invisible prints adorning the otherwise bare walls. A small bar up against the wall seats about half a dozen. And there's outside seating as well. Favorites: Duck Wings Confit (these melt in your mouth, so tender); Cacio & Pepe pasta; Ceviche of the day is always excellent; Pan Seared Foie Gras; Coq a la Biere. Gluten Free/Vegetarian/Vegan options. Tropical cocktails. Outdoor seating.

BLISS KITCHEN
732 Montauk Hwy, Montauk, 631-668-8206
blissmtk.com
WEBSITE DOWN AT PRESSTIME
CUISINE: Café - Deli

DRINKS: No Booze
SERVING: Breakfast (from 7), Lunch & Dinner
PRICE RANGE: $
NEIGHBORHOOD: Montauk
Located in the former Village Deli space, this small café offers a creative menu of Paninis, wraps, burritos, sandwiches, and salads. A few chairs on a rail against the windows if you want to eat here, or in good weather, a patio outside is nice.

BOB'S FISH MARKET
87 N Ferry Rd, Shelter Island, 631-749-0830
No Website
CUISINE: American/Italian
DRINKS: BYOB
SERVING: Breakfast, Lunch, Dinner, Open daily
PRICE RANGE: $$$
This fish market has a restaurant attached and offers casual dining. Lots of fresh fish and daily specials. The lobsters are the best.

BOSTWICK'S CHOWDER HOUSE
277 Pantigo Rd, East Hampton, 631-324-1111
www.bostwickschowderhouse.com
CUISINE: Seafood
DRINKS: Full Bar
SERVING: Lunch, Dinner, Open only Fri - Sun
PRICE RANGE: $$
This seafood eatery offers a great casual setting offering indoor and outdoor dining options. The food is great whether it's the daily catch or one of the chef's specials. Menu favorites include: Fish Tacos and Broiled Sea Scallops. Kids menu available. Soft serve ice cream.

CACI NORTH FORK
56125 Main Rd, Southold, 631-765-4383
www.cacinorthfork.com
CUISINE: Italian
DRINKS: Full bar
SERVING: Lunch & Dinner – Fri – Mon; Dinner only on Tues - Thur
PRICE RANGE: $$$
NEIGHBORHOOD: Southold
Elegant eatery serves a seasonal menu of upscale authentic Italian cuisine. Favorites: Angel hair pasta with lobster, jumbo shrimp with blood orange sauce and Homemade truffle ravioli. The house-made Umbrian pork sausage is quite excellent. Delicious house made bread, pastas and gelato. Favorite dessert: Peach cake. The wine list, while naturally featuring outstanding selections from Italy, does not ignore the local wines of the North Fork. (Check to see if they're

doing their 4-course wine dinners Friday and Sunday during the time you visit. They are beautifully planned and executed.)

CANAL CAFÉ
44 Newtown Rd., Hampton Bays, 631-723-2155
www.thecanalcafe.com
CUISINE: Seafood
DRINKS: Full Bar
SERVING: Lunch & Dinner; closed Tues
PRICE RANGE: $$
NEIGHBORHOOD: Hampton Bays
Very small eatery but it's great eating outside to watch the boats pass by. Menu picks: Fried oysters and Ponzu tuna. Cocktail favorite: Gardiner's Lemonade.

CITTANUOVA
29 Newtown Lane, East Hampton, 631-324-6300
www.cittanuova.com
CUISINE: Italian
DRINKS: Full Bar
SERVING: Lunch, Dinner
PRICE RANGE: $$$
This casual Italian eatery with hints of Milan offers a menu of traditional and contemporary Italian favorites. The front of the house converts in summer into an outdoor seating area that has some of the best people-watching in East Hampton (and that's saying something). There's a more private patio in the back that's also very nice. Menu favorites include: Chicken Milanese and Sorrentina Pizza. Great pasta selection. Bar features TVs for sports fans.

CLAM AND CHOWDER HOUSE AT SALIVAR'S DOCK
470 W Lake Dr, Montauk, 631-668-6252
www.clamandchowderhouse.com
CUISINE: Seafood
DRINKS: Full Bar
SERVING: Breakfast, Lunch & Dinner; closed Tues
PRICE RANGE: $$$
Very popular Montauk eatery with fresh seafood menu and sushi bar. The top deck overlooks the harbor. You can even play games on the upstairs deck while waiting for a table since there's usually a bit of a wait. Great desserts like the chocolate mousse and blueberry cobbler.

COWFISH
258 E Montauk Hwy, Hampton Bays, 631-594-3868
https://cowfishrestaurant.com/
CUISINE: American (New)/Seafood
DRINKS: Full Bar
SERVING: Lunch & Dinner
PRICE RANGE: $$
NEIGHBORHOOD: Hampton Bays
Trendy eatery with a soaring white cathedral style ceiling with wooden beam accents in a big off-kilter modern building that feels like an A-frame structure that was adapted—a great spot I love to visit. I've never seen metal plant-filled pails hanging from a wooden beam used to such positive effect in an interior design. Even if you're inside, lots of windows ensure you don't miss the water views outside. Speaking of outside, there's seating there as well, not

to mention a popular bar during the summer that overlooks the water. Offers a nice menu of American fare and seafood. Menu picks: Lobster roll; Skillet cornbread; Danish Baby Back Ribs; Burgers; NOLA Shrimp (in a Worcestershire reduction sauce that adds a kick). As I said, spectacular waterfront views, children's play area.

DITCH WITCH
40 Deforest Rd, Montauk
No Website
CUISINE: Food Truck
DRINKS: No Booze
SERVING: Open daily
PRICE RANGE: $$$
Located at Ditch Plains Beach, this food truck has been around for years and the menu is written on a beat-up surfboard. Menu favorites include: Turkey & pesto sandwich and the Asian noodle salad. They also serve a variety of Paninis, quesadillas and smoothies.

THE DOCK BAR & GRILL
482 W Lake Dr, Montauk, 631-668-9778
www.thedockmontauk.com
CUISINE: Seafood
DRINKS: Full Bar
SERVING: Lunch, Dinner,
PRICE RANGE: $$
This seafood spot serves fresh off the boat seafood in a local's saloon atmosphere. Great daily specials with treats like the Soft Shell Crab Sandwich. Cash only.

DOCKSIDE BAR & GRILL
26 Bay St, Sag Harbor, 631-725-7100
https://docksidesagharbor.com/
CUISINE: American (Traditional)
DRINKS: Full Bar
SERVING: Lunch & Dinner; Brunch on Sundays; no reservations
PRICE RANGE: $$$
NEIGHBORHOOD: Sag Harbor

Fun dockside eatery offering a perfect spot for lunch or dinner on a summer's day. A chest-high wall separates the small bar from the main dining room, itself quite cozy, with its white tablecloths, stripped and lightly stained wooden floors. This is the old American Legion building converted into a restaurant. Menu picks: Stuffed peppers; Chicken Dumplings; Mussels Milano (dry vermouth & pancetta); and Tuna Wrap with Wasabi Aioli. There was a dinner special one night I particularly liked—the slightly blackened Halibut with a crabmeat guacamole. Vegetarian / Vegan options. Popular for Sunday Brunch.

DOPO LA SPIAGGIA
6 Bay St, Sag Harbor, 631-725-7009
www.dopolaspiaggia.com
CUISINE: Italian
DRINKS: Full Bar
SERVING: Dinner daily; lunch Sat & Sun
PRICE RANGE: $$
NEIGHBORHOOD: Sag Harbor
Formerly Tutto Il Giorno, this spot offers classic Italian fare. Chef Maurizio Marfoglia's menu is classic with favorites like: Cavolini (shaved Brussels sprout Caesar with toasted pine nuts) and Tagliolini (Bay scallops, shrimp, calamari, imported Calabrian chilies and tomato). Reservations recommended.

DURYEA'S LOBSTER DECK
65 Tuthill Rd, Montauk, 631-668-2410
www.duryealobsters.com
CUISINE: Seafood
DRINKS: No Booze
SERVING: Lunch & Dinner; open daily
PRICE RANGE: $$
A very relaxed self-serve eatery featuring paper plates and picnic tables. They've been doing it this way for about 90 years, so something's got to be right. Menu favorites include: Fresh steamed lobsters and Broiled fish. The lobster rolls are of course out of this world, with a lightly laid on mayo. The fish sandwich is also very good, with a buttery quality you can't forget. Great views from the deck. Closes at the end of summer.

EAST HAMPTON GRILL
99 N Main St, East Hampton, 631-329-6666
https://www.easthamptongrill.com/
CUISINE: American
DRINKS: Full Bar
SERVING: Dinner
PRICE RANGE: $$$
NEIGHBORHOOD: East Hampton

Popular upscale eatery in a red-brick building with striped awnings on the main drag in East Hampton has an interior with warm lighting at night, white tablecloth service, a roaring fireplace in the winter, a friendly bar scene. For a month I was out here in the winter, when a lot of places are closed, working on a movie script with a co-writer and we ate lunch or dinner here 4 or 5 days a week. Consistently good. Has a nice selection of American fare and Seafood. Favorites: Lobster Po' Boy; Scallop Salad (something you don't see very often); French Dip; Dover Sole; and the Prime Filet. The burger here is made with a blend of chuck and brisket & served on a homemade bun. Deliciously satisfying. Daily Specials. Save room for the Hot Fudge Sunday dessert.

EAST HAMPTON POINT MARINA
295 3 Mile Harbor Hog Creek Rd, East Hampton, 631 324-9191
www.easthamptonpoint.com
CUISINE: Seafood
DRINKS: Full Bar
SERVING: Breakfast, Lunch, Dinner
PRICE RANGE: $$$

Overlooking Three Mile Harbor, this restaurant serves contemporary American cuisine and fresh seafood. Menu favorites include: Roasted Wild Striped Bass and Dry Boat Halibut. Great daily specials and popular raw bar.

EDGEWATER
295 E Montauk Hwy, Hampton Bays, 631-723-2323
http://www.edgewaterrestaurant.com/
CUISINE: Italian / American
DRINKS: Full Bar
SERVING: Dinner, Lunch & Dinner on Sundays, Closed Mondays
PRICE RANGE: $$$
NEIGHBORHOOD: East Hampton
Gorgeous dark wood beamed interior in this eatery with a great view just east of the Shinnecock Canal offering a menu of classic Italian fare with some American dishes sprinkled around the menu. Favorites: Huge Pasta selection (I had the Orecchiette Broccoli Rabe & Sausage); Farro & Duck Salad; a dozen Pizza offerings (like Eggplant Pizza). Dine in or on the deck overlooking the Bay. Great choice for a special night.

ESTIA'S LITTLE KITCHEN
1615 Bridgehampton / Sag Harbor Tpk., 631-725-1045
www.estias.com
CUISINE: American/Mexican
DRINKS: Beer & Wine Only
SERVING: Breakfast & Lunch; closed Tues
PRICE RANGE: $$$
NEIGHBORHOOD: Sag Harbor
Roadside café that serves eclectic Mexican-American fare. Menu picks: Blueberry pancakes and Poached eggs on Tuscan toast. One of the best brunches in the Hamptons but expect a wait.

FRESNO
8 Fresno Pl, East Hampton, 631-324-8700
www.fresnorestaurant.com
CUISINE: American (New)
DRINKS: Full bar
SERVING: Dinner
PRICE RANGE: $$
NEIGHBORHOOD: East Hampton
Sky-lit eatery offering a menu of creative New American cuisine. Favorites: Orecchiette with Broccoli & Sausage and Grilled Tequila Marinated Duroc Pork Chop. Delicious banana bread for dessert. Great margaritas.

GREY LADY
440 W Lake Dr, Montauk, 631-210-6249
www.greyladymtk.com
CUISINE: Seafood
DRINKS: Full Bar
SERVING: Dinner
PRICE RANGE: $$
NEIGHBORHOOD: Montauk
Sister restaurant to New York City eatery of the same name. Great seafood options in a location just a few feet from Gosman's Dock. There's a 1951 wooden sailboat docked close by that you can charter, with food catered by the restaurant. So you can go out to watch the sunset and return to the restaurant. Menu picks: Lobster roll and Grilled Prime Hanger Steak. Patio and Outdoor dining with a great view.

HIGHWAY RESTAURANT & BAR
290 Montauk Hwy, East Hampton, 631-527-5372
www.highwayrestaurant.com
CUISINE: American (New)
DRINKS: Full Bar
SERVING: Dinner daily, Lunch on weekends
PRICE RANGE: $$$
NEIGHBORHOOD: East Hampton
Great place to eat as everything is good. Menu features popular choices like: Chicken pot pie and Eggplant Parm. Nice selection of wines. Usually crowded so go early.

JACK'S STIR BREW COFFEE
146 Montauk Hwy, Amagansett, 631-267-5555
www.jacksstirbrew.com
CUISINE: Coffee & Tea
DRINKS: No Booze
SERVING: 6:30 a.m. – 5 p.m. daily
PRICE RANGE: $$
NEIGHBORHOOD: Amagansett
Serving a perfect cup of coffee and delicious baked organic vegan donuts, this is a locals' favorite. Here you'll find a variety of healthy vegan baked goods and shelves of brand name products. Breakfast and lunch offering great vegetarian options to dine in or for take-out.

JUE LAN CLUB
268 Elm St, Southampton, 631-353-3610
www.juelanclub.com
CUISINE: Chinese
DRINKS: Full Bar

SERVING: Dinner daily, Brunch on Sat; late-night lounge open Thurs - Sat
PRICE RANGE: $$$
NEIGHBORHOOD: Southampton
Don't like Chinese food? This is the perfect spot for you. This place serves signature dishes from its NYC flagship location like: Drunken Sea Bass and Chicken Satay. Located in the former Circo Southampton location, this place also brings a new energy to Southampton nightlife with its signature Asian dishes, nightlife and art exhibitions.

LOBSTER ROLL
1980 Montauk Hwy, Amagansett, 631-267-3740
https://lobsterroll.com/
CUISINE: Seafood/American (Traditional)
DRINKS: No Booze
SERVING: Lunch, Dinner Fri – Sun, Closed Wednesdays
PRICE RANGE: $$
NEIGHBORHOOD: East Hampton
Popular family restaurant known for its huge lunch cowd. They've made some effort to give the place a "nautical" feel, with some netting strung here and there, a couple of stuffed fish hanging on the walls, but it's basically a good old-fashioned lobster shack. Plenty of outdoor seating under an awning. Favorites: Grandma's Crabcakes; Steamed Mussels; Char-broiled Tuna Steak Sandwich; and of course the Lobster Roll, made to perfection. Take-out available.

LT BURGER
62 Main St, Sag Harbor, 631-899-4646
www.ltburger.com
CUISINE: Burgers/American
DRINKS: Full Bar
SERVING: Breakfast, Lunch, Dinner, Closed Sundays
PRICE RANGE: $$

Chef Laurent Tourondel offers a menu of classic burgers using local ingredients.
Great appetizers and burgers like the Mecox cheddar burger and the LT backyard cheeseburger. Don't forget the signature milkshakes and delicious dessert

selection including the peanut butter and milk chocolate s'mores.

NATURALLY GOOD FOODS & CAFÉ
779 Montauk Hwy (NY 27), Montauk, 631-668-9030

www.naturallygoodcafe.com
CUISINE: Health food/Gluten-free
DRINKS: Beer & Wine
SERVING: Breakfast, Lunch & Dinner
PRICE RANGE: $$
Health food store that offers a full service breakfast and lunch menu. Favorites include: smoothies, salads, and veggie burgers, burritos, and vegan baked goods. My favorite sandwich: The Bruce, which is tuna salad sandwich with avocado and cheddar cheese.

NAVY BEACH
16 Navy Rd, Montauk, 631-668-6868
www.navybeach.com
CUISINE: Seafood/American
DRINKS: Full Bar
SERVING: Fri, Sat, Sun
PRICE RANGE: $$$
This locals' favorite beachfront restaurant serves casual seafood in a comfortable setting. Menu favorites include: Jumbo Lump Crab Cake and

Buttermilk Fried Chicken. Take a seat at the 35-foot antique wooden bar for one of their signature cocktails or one of the many domestic and imported beers. I find this place to be just as good for lunch or dinner.

NICK & TONI'S
136 N Main St, East Hampton, 631-324-3550
www.nickandtonis.com
CUISINE: Pizza/Italian
DRINKS: Full Bar
SERVING: Lunch, Dinner, Closed Mon & Tues
PRICE RANGE: $$$$
Perhaps you've heard of this place, as it's one of the most popular spots in the Hamptons. With the feeling of a Tuscan farmhouse, this hot non-smoking restaurant offers a great dining experience with an impressive selection of wines. If you can get a

reservation, then you'll enjoy such favorites as Penne alla Vecchia Bettola and the Fazzoletti with Baby Artichoke, Sorrel, and Fontina. Seasonal menu using fresh produce grown in their own garden.

NOAH'S
136 Front St, Greenport, 631-477-6720
www.chefnoahs.com
CUISINE: American (New)
DRINKS: Full bar
SERVING: Dinner, Lunch Fri – Sun; closed on Wed
PRICE RANGE: $$$
NEIGHBORHOOD: Greenpoint
Storefront eatery offering a farm-to-table menu of small plates with a raw bar. (The littleneck clams come from nearby Peconic Bay.) Favorites: Short rib rigatoni and Duck liver mousse. For dessert try the Spicy Mexican chocolate sorbet.

PELLEGRINO'S PIZZA BAR & RESTAURANT
1271 Noyack Rd, Southampton, 631-283-9742
http://www.pellegrinospizzabar.com/
CUISINE: Italian/Pizza
DRINKS: Full Bar
SERVING: Dinner; closed Tues & Weds.
PRICE RANGE: $$$
NEIGHBORHOOD: Southampton
Set in a converted house, this upscale eatery offers a menu of contemporary Northern Italian cuisine, though the centerpiece is the brick wood-fired oven where they make some of the best pizzas you're going to find anywhere in these parts. But there's more than pizza. Seared calamari, steamers,

charcuteri boards. They have a half dozen "red" pizzas" and a half dozen "white." Favorites: Meatball pizza and House burgers. Full bar with nice selection of crafted beers. Kid friendly. Gluten-free options.

PIERRE'S
2468 Main St, Bridgehampton, 631-537-5110
www.pierresbridgehampton.com
CUISINE: French
DRINKS: Full bar
SERVING: Breakfast/Lunch/Dinner
PRICE RANGE: $$$
NEIGHBORHOOD: Bridgehampton
Cozy eatery offering up creative versions of French classics and seafood dishes. Favorites: Soft Shell Crab and Roasted boned chicken. You must try the crustless apple pie with vanilla ice cream. There's an excellent bakery up front.

RICK'S CRABBY COWBOY CAFÉ
435 E Lake Dr, Montauk, 631-668-3200
crabbycowboy.com
CUISINE: Seafood/Barbeque
DRINKS: Full Bar
SERVING: Lunch & Dinner
PRICE RANGE: $$
NEIGHBORHOOD: Montauk
Family-friendly beachside eatery offers a creative menu of local seafood and Barbeque. Menu picks: Lobster Roll and Local striped bass. Try their Crabby Bakes (either lobster, crab legs or ribeye steak). Locals' hangout.

RUMBA
43 Canoe Place Rd, Hampton Bays, 631-594-3544
https://rumbahamptonbays.com/
CUISINE: Caribbean/Seafood
DRINKS: Full Bar
SERVING: Lunch & Dinner
PRICE RANGE: $$$
NEIGHBORHOOD: Long Island
Caribbean-style eatery with an island décor and leaf-shaped paddle pans slowly twirling above in a niche in the arched wooden ceiling. They have a dock across the street where boats can pull in. Some outdoor seating at picnic tables or at a rail on a deck overlooking the water. Super casual, and lots of fun. "Caribbean" flavored menu with handcrafted rum cocktails. Great for dinner or snacking. Favorites: Dominican Ribs (they're famous for these because of the sweet chili soy glaze, but I find them to be too sweet); Duck empanadas; a big selection of salads, like Crab cake salad, or the Jumbo Scallop & Papaya Salad; Tacos (about 6 kinds); Pork tenderloin (coconut finish); several burgers.

SERAFINA
104 North Main St, East Hampton, 631-267-3500
www.serafinarestaurant.com
CUISINE: Italian
DRINKS: Full Bar
SERVING: Lunch (Fri- Sun), Dinner, Closed Mondays
PRICE RANGE: $$$

This eatery is a favorite of locals and visitors alike who enjoy the varied selection of brick-oven pizzas (they have over 20 pizza selections, some very creative) and risottos. The menu includes the traditional pizza margherita and favorites like Lobster Carpaccio, Goat Cheese Salad, and a selection of seafood, poultry, and meat dishes. Their homemade desserts include tiramisu, berry tart, and a delicious Italian cheesecake. Has a lively bar scene.

SOUTH EDISON
17 S Edison St, Montauk, 631-668-4200
www.southedison.com
CUISINE: Seafood
DRINKS: Full Bar
SERVING: Lunch, Dinner,
PRICE RANGE: $$$
Chef Todd Mitgang offers a creative menu featuring local seafood and produce. The bar features a large selection of wines and beers. Menu favorites include: Seared Yellowfin Tuna and Black & Blue Local Sea Scallops.

STONE CREEK INN
405 Montauk Hwy, East Quogue, 631-653-6770
www.stonecreekinn.com
CUISINE: French/American (New)
DRINKS: Full bar
SERVING: Dinner
PRICE RANGE: $$$$

NEIGHBORHOOD: East Quogue
Set in a grand Victorian house, this eatery serves high-end French inspired cuisine with the extravagantly high prices to go along with it. Favorites: Grilled Octopus appetizer and Filet mignon. Nice bar area for cocktails before you dine so you can steel yourself before you get the bill, and after dining, when you can get a Cognac to settle your nerves after paying it.

SUNSET BEACH
35 Shore Road, Shelter Island, Long Island, 617-749-2001
sunsetbeachli.com
CUISINE: French
DRINKS: Full Bar
SERVING: Breakfast, Lunch & Dinner
PRICE RANGE: $$
NEIGHBORHOOD: Long Island
Located in Sunset Beach Hotel, this French-inspired bistro serves favorites like New York strip steak and daily "catch of the day." Dine on the deck and tan while you're eating or inside where it's cool. The connecting bar attracts a local crowd who come for the diverse selection of DJs.

TOPPING ROSE HOUSE
One Bridgehampton-Sag Harbor Turnpike, Bridgehampton, 631-537-0870
www.toppingrosehouse.com
CUISINE: American (New)
DRINKS: Full Bar
SERVING: Breakfast, Lunch & Dinner

PRICE RANGE: $$$$
The extremely fine restaurant here offers a menu of locally sourced New American and farm-to-table dishes. Very chic surroundings. Menu favorites include: Lamb pancetta and Saffron garganelli with lobster. Nice wine pairings. Creative desserts.

TOUCH OF VENICE
28350 Main Rd, Cutchogue, 631-298-5851
www.touchofvenice.com
CUISINE: Italian/Seafood
DRINKS: Full bar
SERVING: Lunch & Dinner
PRICE RANGE: $$$
NEIGHBORHOOD: Cutchogue
Relaxed eatery serving creative Italian classics and seafood dishes. Favorites: Eggplant Rollatini and Veal Parmigiana. Don't leave without tasting their famous Italian cheesecake. Wine list includes Italian

classics and local North Fork wines. Locals' favorite with live music on Friday nights.

UNION CANTINA
40 Bowden Square, Southampton, 631-377-3500
www.unioncantina.net
CUISINE: Mexican
DRINKS: Full Bar
SERVING: Dinner; closed Mon & Tues
PRICE RANGE: $$
NEIGHBORHOOD: Southampton
Set in the former Publick House space, this new eatery offers traditional Mexican fare including quesadillas, deconstructed enchiladas, and tacos. Creative cocktails featuring things like fermented agave. They have 3 bars here. One of them is the 400 Rabits Tequila Bar offering about 100 different tequilas.

VINE STREET CAFÉ
41 S Ferry Rd, Shelter Island, 631-749-3210
vinestreetcafe.com
CUISINE: American (New)/Italian/Asian Fusion
DRINKS: Full Bar
SERVING: Dinner; closed Tues & Wed
PRICE RANGE: $$$
NEIGHBORHOOD: Shelter Island
Set in a remodeled American cottage with a food shop attached. Great menu focusing on local produce, seafood and wines. Menu picks: Calamari Salad and Bolognese Pasta. A celebrity hangout. Reservations recommended.

Chapter 4
NIGHTLIFE

MONTAUK BREWING CO
62 S Erie Ave, Montauk, 631-668-8471
www.montaukbrewingco.com
Known for their quality beer, this place features an intimate taproom. Note, this is not really a bar but a brewery. My favorite of their offerings, "Summer Ale."

SLOPPY TUNA
148 S. Emerson Avenue, Montauk, 631-647-8000
www.lisloppytuna.com
This very friendly two-level beachside bar attracts the hipsters during the summer season. The décor is very beach-inspired surf bungalow that offers several party areas and live DJs spinning until 4 a.m.

SOUTHAMPTON SOCIAL CLUB
256 Elm Street, Southampton, 631-287-1400
www.southamptonsocialclub.com
Formerly Madam Tong's space, this new garden-like environment features outdoor seating and private cabanas. Chef Scott Kampf provides the menu but this is one of the Hampton's premiere nightlife destinations. Some of the hottest summer events are hosted here. On Thur – Sat during the summer guests can enjoy some of the hottest DJs in the industry.

THE STEPHEN TALKHOUSE
161 Main Street, Amagansett, 631-267-3117
www.stephentalkhouse.com
This place opened in 1970 and has set the standard for live music in the area and continues to be the East End's most popular and famous bar. Very laid-back atmosphere with outstanding music. Prices vary depending on the act.

Chapter 5
WHAT TO SEE & DO

GUILD HALL
158 Main St, East Hampton, 631-324-0806
www.guildhall.org
Open since 1931, this place has earned the reputation as the primary cultural center on the East End, offering programs in art, education, literature, and theater. Guild Hall has presented exhibitions of well-known artists like Willem de Kooning and Jackson Pollock. Visit the website for their year-round schedule of activities.

LIGHTHOUSE MONTAUK POINT
2000 New York 27, Montauk, 631-668-2544
www.montauklighthouse.com
Completed on November 5, 1796, this is the oldest lighthouse in New York State and still serves as an aid to navigation. This beautiful historic site is a favorite location for weddings and special events. Tours available. Minimal admission fee.

LONGHOUSE RESERVE
133 Hands Creek Rd, East Hampton, 631-329-3568
www.longhouse.org
The LongHouse Reserve, a non-profit art museum and sculpture garden features sixteen acres of gardens, water features, and over 90 sculptures by such eminent artists as Dale Chihuly, Buckminster Fuller, Yoko Ono and Willem de Kooning. The venue also features temporary exhibitions. It was founded by textile designer Jack Lenor Larsen, who, as I recall, used to live here.

POLLOCK-KRASNER HOUSE AND STUDY CENTER
830 Springs-Fireplace Rd, East Hampton, 631-324-4929

www.pkhouse.org
Built in 1879, this National Historic Landmark is the former home and studio of artists Jackson Pollock and

Lee Krasner. Pollock bought this place in 1946 for about $5,000 (doesn't that make you ill?). The house contains furnishings and artifacts from the lives of the two artists. Paintings by Pollock and prints of both artists are displayed including a revolving exhibition of work. Tours of the studio and house are available during the summer season. You have to put on little foot booties when you go into the barn because you're walking on the splattered paint that Pollock dripped when he was flinging the paint at his big canvases. Though I will never "understand" his work—to me it looks incredibly stupid and indulgent—I found my visit here more than worthwhile. Fascinating, really.

WÖLFFER ESTATE VINEYARD
139 Sagg Rd, Sagaponack, 631-537-5106
www.wolffer.com
Known as one of the best vineyards in the northeast featuring European style grapes grown in U.S. The 55-acre estate is part of a 175-acre estate complete with boarding stables, indoor jumping ring, and a Grand Prix field. Here you'll find an excellent selection of world-class wines. The Estate offers a variety of events including: wine tastings, yoga, a farmer's market, evening socials, a pig roast, art events, and an annual Harvest Party.

Chapter 6
BEACHES

Details on parking fees and other beach rules and regulations an be found at:

Long Island Convention & Visitors Bureau
www.discoverlongisland.com

ATLANTIC AVENUE BEACH
4 Atlantic Ave, Amagansett
This is a great beach to visit if you don't have a village permit. There's a concession stand with a nice variety of beach snacks. Nice family beach and facilities include restrooms and lifeguards. Parking fee.

COOPERS BEACH
268 Meadow Lane, Southampton, 631-283-0247
This scenic beach (recently voted No. 2 best beach in the U.S.) stretches for 500 feet along the Atlantic's shore. The beach offers a concession stand (usually has a long line, so be smart and bring a packed lunch with you), chair and umbrella rentals, bathrooms and fresh water showers. Daily parking permit that runs is expensive.

DITCH PLAINS BEACH
Montauk Peninsula, Montauk
This beach is known as the local surfing mecca and is a popular spot for families during the summer. Facilities include restrooms and a concession stand. Parking fee if you don't have a town beach-parking pass.

MAIN BEACH
Ocean Ave, East Hampton
This is the Hamptons' main beach and is usually littered with hipsters, celebrities, and super models during season. Best to bike here as the parking fee is

quite hefty. (On weekends, you can park even if you want to pay. You have to walk or ride bikes.)

SAGG MAIN BEACH
Sagg Main St., Sagaponack, 631-728–8585
This popular beach offers 1,500 feet of white sand. Popular for volleyball matches. Facilities include: showers, restrooms, concession stand, and picnic tables. Activities available: fishing and surfing. Parking fee without parking permit. Wheelchair accessible.

SHELL BEACH
Shelter Island
Located on the southwest corner of the island in West Neck Harbor. This half-mile long beach is located on a long peninsula and is generally less populated than the other beaches as its undeveloped and has no amenities.

WESTHAMPTON DUNES
Southampton Town Park
Located off Dune Road in the middle of West Hampton Dunes. This beach offers 400 feet of shoreline that's ideal for sunbathing and swimming. Facilities include lifeguards and restrooms. Parking fee without a Town Resident Permit.

Chapter 7
SHOPPING & SERVICES

AMAGANSETT SEAFOOD STORE
517 Montauk Hwy, Amagansett, 631-267-6015
www.amagansettseafoodstore.net
CUISINE: Seafood Market
DRINKS: Beer & Wine
SERVING: Open daily
PRICE RANGE: $$$
Known for selling the freshest fish in the area. Shop for items to take home or snack here. Great selection of seafood like lobster rolls, fish tacos, seaweed salad and even lobster mac and cheese. A locals' hangout on Saturdays.

BRAHMIN LEATHER
58 Jobs Lane, Southampton, 613-287-2386
www.brahmin.com
This Massachusetts-based leather handbag company has opened a Hamptons location offering their impressive line of handbags.

BROOKS BROTHERS
48 Main St, Southampton, 631-287-3936
www.brooksbrothers.com
Everyone knows Brooks Brothers and what better location for this store than the Hamptons? This is Brooks Brothers Country Club where everything is sporty and casual and more preppy (if that's possible). Yes, they have striped oxford button downs and blue blazers, but also fashionable beach wear.

CYNTHIA ROWLEY
MEMORY HOTEL
696 Montauk Highway, Montauk, 631-668-8077
www.cynthiarowley.com
This is a tiny store is filled with Cynthia Rowley collections including shoes and handbags. The store also offers home and gardening items and Rowley's surf line including her customized Meyerhoffer surfboard. Here you'll also find unique necklaces and perfumes from Morocco.

ELIE TAHARI
1 Main St, East Hampton, (631) 329-8883
www.elietahari.com
This shop specializes in women's designer fashions, office wear, and evening wear.

JOHN VARVATOS
54 Newtown Lane, East Hampton, 631-324-4440
www.johnvarvatos.com

This shop features the luxury brand and collections from John Varvatos. The styles are eclectic and fashionable. Here you'll find men's fashions, shoes, accessories, and fragrances.

MAIN BEACH SURF & SPORT
352 Montauk Highway, Wainscott, 631-537-2716
www.mainbeach.com
This is your one-stop-shopping stop for all your surfing and water sports gear. Here you'll find paddleboards, surfboards, kayaks, wetsuits, carracks, beachwear, athletic apparel and accessories. Lines carried include: Patagonia, Hobie, Quicksilver, Bark, Surf Tech, Kialoa, and Ocean Kayak. Surf lessons, paddleboard classes, and kayak tours are also offered as well as kayak fishing tours, and guide services. MBX Surf Camp for Kids offered seasonally.

MELET MERCANTILE
102 Industrial Rd, Montauk, 631-668-2843
www.meletmercantile.com
Regional retail outlet and event space. Here you can find surfboards, vintage rock concert t-shirts, maps, and other interesting finds in this little treasure chest. Owner used to buy vintage items for Ralph Lauren. Open daily 11-7, May – Oct.

PIERRE'S MARKET
542 Sagg Main Street, Sagaponack, 631-296-8400
www.pierresbridgehampton.com
CUISINE: Deli
DRINKS: No Booze
SERVING: Open daily
PRICE RANGE: $
This deli serves delicious egg sandwiches (until 11 a.m.) and other treats like bagels, muffins, pastries, homemade salads, and curried chicken. A menu favorite is the homemade meatloaf sandwich. Gluten-free options available. Great place to buy t-shirts and hats.

ROBERTA FREYMANN
21 Main St, East Hampton, 631-329-5828
www.robertarollerrabbit.com
The line features women's ready-to-wear, outerwear, jewelry and accessories. Everything is designed or discovered by Roberta.

ROUND SWAMP FARM
184 Three Mile Harbor Rd, East Hampton, 631-324-4438
www.roundswampfarm.com
This is a unique combination of a country market, fish market, and bakery that sells freshly made products, local seafood, produce, and home-cooked specialties. Here you'll find delicious treats from chicken fingers to homemade cookies and scones. This is a good place to buy lunch so you don't have to wait in line at the beach concessions.

SURF BAZAAR AT THE SURF LODGE
183 S Edgemere St, Montauk, 631-668-1035
www.thesurfbazaar.com
Perfect shopping spot for the summer traveler as you'll find a unique collection of beach clothing and

accessories. The shop carries the collections of over 30 designers. There's a line of perforated tanks that read "Surf," a collaboration of owner – designer Bethany Mayer and Love Leather.

TORY SPORT
47 Newtown Lane, East Hampton, 631-907-9150
www.toryburch.com
This boutique is filled with Bohemian-inspired colorful fashions. Here you'll find ready-to-wear, shoes, handbags, and accessories.

URBAN ZEN
16 Main St, Sag Harbor, 631 725 6176
https://urbanzen.com
This new boutique was created and designed by fashion icon Donna Karan. The shop has a mission to create change and empower children through Karan's

fashions, accessories and jewelry. The Sag Harbor shop also hosts trunk shows and book signings.

WHALEBONE CREATIVE
65 Tuthill Rd, Montauk
https://shopwhalebone.com
A unique shop offers lifestyle based clothing including graphic t-shirts and surf-inspired fashions. Shortboarders hanging out on Ditch Plains Beach prize the limited-edition hoodies and tanks offered by owner Jesse James Joeckel. Be sure to check the waves before you come here. "If the waves are good, nobody works."

INDEX

1

1770 HOUSE RESTAURANT & INN, 17

7

75 MAIN, 34

A

ALMOND, 35
AMAGANSETT, 13
AMAGANSETT SEAFOOD, 35, 81
American, 49, 61
American (New), 51, 63
American Hotel, 15
AMERICAN HOTEL, 18, 35
ARBOR, 36
Asian Fusion, 63
ATLANTIC AVENUE BEACH, 76
ATLANTIC HOTEL, 18

B

BABETTE'S, 36
BAKER HOUSE 1650, 19
Barbeque, 57
BARON'S COVE, 20
BEACH BAKERY CAFÉ, 37
BEACH PLUM RESORT, 22
BEACHCOMBER RESORT, 21

BISTRO ÉTÉ, 38
BLISS KITCHEN, 38
BOB'S FISH MARKET, 39
BOSTWICK'S CHOWDER HOUSE, 40
BOWEN'S BY THE BAYS, 23
BRAHMIN LEATHER, 82
BRIDGEHAMPTON, 12
BROOKS BROTHERS, 82
BUTLER'S MANOR, A, 23

C

CACI NORTH FORK, 40
Cafe, 38
CANAL CAFÉ, 41
Chinese, 51
CITTANUOVA, 41
CLAM AND CHOWDER HOUSE, 42
Claude's, 31
Coffee & Tea, 51
COOPERS BEACH, 76
COWFISH, 42
CROW'S NEST INN, 24
CYNTHIA ROWLEY, 82

D

DITCH PLAINS BEACH, 77
DITCH WITCH, 43
DOCK BAR & GRILL, 44
DOCKSIDE BAR & GRILL, 44
DOPO LA SPIAGGIA, 45

DRIFTWOOD ON THE OCEAN, 25
DURYEA'S LOBSTER DECK, 46

E

EAST HAMPTON, 13
EAST HAMPTON GRILL, 47
EAST HAMPTON POINT, 48
EDGEWATER, 49
ELIE TAHARI, 83
ELL & ANCHOR, 37
ESTIA'S LITTLE KITCHEN, 49

F

French, 35, 61
FRESNO, 50

G

Gluten-free, 54
GREY LADY, 50
GUILD HALL, 70

H

HAMPTON BAYS, 11
HAMPTON JITNEY, 10
HAMPTON MAID INN, 24
HARBORSIDE MOTEL, 26
Health food, 54
HEDGES INN, 27
HELICOPTER SERVICE, 10
HIGHWAY, 51

I

Indonesian, 42, 44
INN AT WINDMILL LANE, 28
Italian, 45, 63

J

JACK'S STIR BREW COFFEE, 51
JOHN VARVATOS, 83
JUE LAN CLUB, 51

L

LIGHTHOUSE, 71
LOBSTER ROLL, 52
Long Island Convention & Visitors Bureau, 75
LONG ISLAND RAILROAD, 10
LONGHOUSE RESERVE, 72
LT BURGER, 53

M

MAIDSTONE, 29
MAIN BEACH, 77
MAIN BEACH SURF & SPORT, 84
Mediterranean, 36
MELET MERCANTILE, 85
MEMORY HOTEL, 82
Mexican, 49, 63
MONTAUK, 14
MONTAUK BEACH HOUSE, 30
MONTAUK BREWING CO, 65
MONTAUK YACHT CLUB, 30

N

NATURALLY GOOD FOODS & CAFÉ, 53
NAVY BEACH, 54
NICK & TONI'S, 55
NOAH'S, 56

P

PELLEGRINO'S PIZZA BAR & RESTAURANT, 56
PIERRE'S, 57
PIERRE'S MARKET, 85
POLLOCK-KRASNER HOUSE, 72

Q

QUOGUE, 11

R

RICK'S CRABBY COWBOY CAFÉ, 57
ROBERTA FREYMANN, 85
ROUND SWAMP FARM, 86
RUMBA, 58
RUSCHMEYER'S, 30

S

SAG HARBOR, 14
SAGAPONACK, 13
SAGG MAIN BEACH, 78
Seafood, 36, 41, 42, 46, 50, 57
SERAFINA, 59
SHELL BEACH, 79
SHELTER ISLAND, 15
SLOPPY TUNA, 66
SOLE EAST RESORT, 31
SOUTH EDISON, 60
SOUTHAMPTON, 12
SOUTHAMPTON INN, 31
SOUTHAMPTON SOCIAL CLUB, 67
STEPHEN TALKHOUSE, 68
STONE CREEK INN, 60
SUNSET BEACH, 31, 61
SURF BAZAAR AT THE SURF LODGE, 86
SURF LODGE, 32

T

TOPPING ROSE HOUSE, 33, 61
TORY SPORT, 87
TOUCH OF VENICE, 62

U

UNION CANTINA, 63
URBAN ZEN, 87

V

Vegan, 36
VINE STREET CAFÉ, 63

W

WAINSCOTT, 13
WATER MILL, 12
WESTHAMPTON, 11
WESTHAMPTON DUNES, 79
WHALEBONE CREATIVE, 88
WÖLFFER ESTATE VINEYARD, 74

Other Books by the Same Author

Andrew Delaplaine has written in widely varied fields: screenplays, novels (adult and juvenile), travel writing, journalism. His books are available in quality bookstores, libraries, as well as all online retailers.

JACK HOUSTON ST. CLAIR POLITICAL THRILLERS

On Election night, as China and Russia mass soldiers on their common border in preparation for war, there's a tie in the Electoral College that forces the decision for

President into the House of Representatives as mandated by the Constitution. The incumbent Republican President, working through his Aide for Congressional Liaison, uses the Keystone File, which contains dirt on every member of Congress, to blackmail members into supporting the Republican candidate. The action runs from Election Night in November to Inauguration Day on January 20. Jack Houston St. Clair runs a small detective agency in Miami. His father is Florida Governor Sam Houston St. Clair, the Republican candidate. While he tries to help his dad win the election, Jack also gets hired to follow up on some suspicious wire transfers involving drug smugglers, leading him to a sunken narco-sub off Key West that has $65 million in cash in its hull.

AFTER THE OATH: DAY ONE
AFTER THE OATH: MARCH WINDS
WEDDING AT THE WHITE HOUSE

Only three months have passed since Sam Houston St. Clair was sworn in as the new President, but a lot has happened. Returning from Vienna where he met with Russian and Chinese diplomats, Sam is making his way back to Flagler Hall in Miami, his first trip home since being inaugurated. Son Jack is in the midst of turmoil of his own back in Miami, dealing with various dramas, not the least of which is his increasing alienation from Babylon Fuentes and his growing attraction to the seductive Lupe Rodriguez. Fernando Pozo addresses new problems as he struggles to expand Cuba's secret operations in the U.S., made even more difficult as U.S.-Cuban relations thaw. As his father returns home, Jack knows Sam will find as much trouble at home as he did in Vienna.

WANT 3 **FREE** NOVELS?

If you like these writers--
Vince Flynn, Brad Thor, Tom Clancy, James Patterson, David Baldacci, John Grisham, Brad Meltzer, Daniel Silva, Don DeLillo

If you like these TV series –
House of Cards, Scandal, West Wing, The Good Wife, Madam Secretary, Designated Survivor

You'll love the **unputdownable** series about Jack Houston St. Clair, with political intrigue, romance, suspense.

Besides writing travel books, I've written political thrillers for many years. I want you to read my work!
Send me an email and I'll send you a link where you can download the 3 books, absolutely FREE.

andrewdelaplaine@mac.com

www.ingramcontent.com/pod-product-compliance
Lightning Source LLC
Chambersburg PA
CBHW020016050426
42450CB00005B/502